Pebble® Plus

Let's Take a FIELD TRIP

T0080820

A LIBRARY FIELD TRIP

by Isabel Martin

Consulting editor:
Gail Saunders-Smith, PhD

Content Consultant:
Susan M. Bartle
School Library System
Coordinator
Erie 2-Chautauqua-
Cattaraugus BOCES,
Fredonia, NY

CAPSTONE PRESS
a capstone imprint

Pebble Plus is published by Capstone Press,
1710 Roe Crest Drive, North Mankato, Minnesota 56003
www.capstonepub.com

Copyright © 2015 by Capstone Press, a Capstone imprint. All rights reserved. No part of
this publication may be reproduced in whole or in part, or stored in a retrieval system,
or transmitted in any form or by any means, electronic, mechanical, photocopying,
recording, or otherwise, without written permission of the publisher.

Library of Congress Cataloging-in-Publication Data
Martin, Isabel, 1977–
 A library field trip / by Isabel Martin.
  pages cm. — (Pebble plus. Let's take a field trip)
Summary: "Simple text and full-color photographs take readers on a virtual field
trip to the library"—Provided by publisher.
 Audience: Ages 4–8.
 Audience: K to grade 3.
 Includes bibliographical references and index.
 ISBN 978-1-4914-2097-3 (library binding) — ISBN 978-1-4914-2315-8 (pbk.) —
ISBN 978-1-4914-2338-7 (ebook PDF)
 1. Libraries—Juvenile literature. I. Title.

Z665.5.M365 2015
027.4—dc23   2014032321

Editorial Credits
Nikki Bruno Clapper, editor; Juliette Peters, designer;
Gina Kammer, media researcher; Tori Abraham, production specialist

Photo Credits
Alamy: Tetra Images, LLC, (top) 13; Capstone Studio: Karon Dubke, (left) 5, (middle left) 9;
Getty Images: Goodboy Picture Company, (right) 21; Shutterstock: Andresr, (middle right)
cover, DavidPinoPhotography, cover, 2, 22, Erika J Mitchell, cover, michaeljung, cover,
Monkey Business Images, 11, 15, Orhan Cam, back cover, 1, Tyler Olson, cover, 3, 7, 17, 19

Note to Parents and Teachers

The Let's Take a Field Trip set supports national curriculum standards for social studies related
to institutions, communities, and civic practices. This book describes and illustrates a class field
trip to a library. The images support early readers in understanding the text. The repetition
of words and phrases helps early readers learn new words. This book also introduces early
readers to subject-specific vocabulary words, which are defined in the Glossary section. Early
readers may need assistance to read some words and to use the Table of Contents, Glossary,
Read More, Internet Sites, Critical Thinking Using the Common Core, and Index sections of
the book.

Printed and bound in China. 5070

TABLE OF CONTENTS

A SPECIAL SCHOOL DAY

Today is field trip day.

Your class is going to

your town's public library!

AT THE LIBRARY

Many people use the library.

They sit at tables and

read books quietly.

They also use computers.

The library is filled

with shelves of books.

Fiction books tell stories.

Nonfiction books are full

of information.

Some people read books for fun. Other people want to find answers to questions. Books and computers help them do research.

LIBRARIANS ARE DETECTIVES!

How do you find the
right books? Ask a librarian.
Librarians are detectives.
They help you find
answers to your questions.

Librarians read books

out loud during story time.

Children listen to the story.

Librarians and other
workers organize the library.
They put books in order
on the shelves. Now visitors
can find books easily.

CHECKING OUT

Visitors can check out,

or borrow, library materials.

You can take home books

or DVDs. All you need is

a library card.

Field trips to the library are fun. You can learn to be a detective too. Visit again soon!

GLOSSARY

check out—to borrow library materials by taking them to a clerk at the counter

detective—a person who solves mysteries or collects information for people

fiction—written works about characters and events that aren't real

field trip—a class visit for learning something new at a place outside school

library card—a card with a person's name and library number printed on it; people use library cards to borrow materials from the library

materials—the library items that people use or check out; books, magazines, newspapers, videos, and DVDs are library materials

nonfiction—written works about real people, places, objects, or events

organize—to arrange things neatly and in order

public—having to do with people in general; a public place is one where everyone can go

research—the process of studying and learning about a subject

READ MORE

Gorman, Jacqueline Laks. *Librarians.* People in My Community. New York: Gareth Stevens Pub., 2010.

Keogh, Josie. *A Trip to the Library.* Powerkids Readers: My Community. New York: PowerKids Press, 2013.

Piehl, Janet. *Explore the Library.* Library Smarts. Minneapolis: Lerner Publications Company, 2014.

INTERNET SITES

FactHound offers a safe, fun way to find Internet sites related to this book. All of the sites on FactHound have been researched by our staff.

Here's all you do:

Visit *www.facthound.com*

Type in this code: 9781491420973

Super-cool stuff! Check out projects, games and lots more at **www.capstonekids.com**

CRITICAL THINKING
USING THE COMMON CORE

1. What kinds of materials can you check out at the library?
(Key Ideas and Details)

2. Look at the pictures. What do people like to do at the library?
(Integration of Knowledge and Ideas)

INDEX

Word Count: 164
Grade: 1
Early-Intervention Level: 16